D. J. NORTON'S pictorial survey of
RAILWAYS
IN THE
WEST MIDLANDS

PART THREE
LMS MIDLAND DIVISION
Former Birmingham & Gloucester Railway and later lines connecting to it.

by R. J. ESSERY
With contributions from T. J. EDGINGTON

WILD SWAN PUBLICATIONS

ISBN 978 1 905184 52 1

D.J. NORTON

D.J. Norton – Dennis John Norton – was born in Birmingham in March 1930. He developed an interest in railways early in his life and started photographing locomotives, stations and lines at the age of 17, just as British Railways were taking over from the 'Big Four'. His interest continued right up to his premature death as the result of an asthma attack in August 1965. Throughout this time his camera was primarily pointed at subjects related to the LMS Company. He held a lineside pass but his concept of 'lineside' seems at odds with what the authorities intended. Standing in the middle of main lines, walking through tunnels, and even climbing signal posts, were frequent activities. The result of all this disobedience is a collection of photographs containing many unique and unusual views.

Unfortunately, D.J. Norton did not visit every location within the area we have tried to cover, so if we have not included a location, it is simply because he did not take any pictures of it. In Part I we have acknowledged his various 'railway friends' who helped him to achieve a pictorial record of the railway scene in the West Midlands.

D. J. Norton's complete photograph collection.

Designed by Paul Karau
Printed by Amadeus Press, Cleckheaton

Published by
WILD SWAN PUBLICATIONS LTD.
1-3 Hagbourne Road, Didcot, Oxon, OX11 8DP

CONTENTS

BIRMINGHAM & GLOUCESTER RAILWAY VIA CAMP HILL 5

THE LONGBRIDGE TO HALESOWEN BRANCH 89

BARNT GREEN TO REDDITCH 105

INTRODUCTION

When work on this project began, the original intention was to publish a single volume of D. J. Norton's pictures, but as we progressed it became clear that the number and quality of pictures available was more than could comfortably be accommodated within a single volume, so we decided that a three-part work would be more sensible. It was clear that it should be centred upon Birmingham, the United Kingdom's second city, and show the old LMS lines from the final year of the LMS until 1963 when D.J. Norton moved to Ledbury. It was also clear there would not be any GWR pictures; as far as we can see, he did not photograph anything belonging to that company while he lived in Birmingham.

The first part of this trilogy deals with the lines of the old London & North Western Railway, which after 1923 became the Western Division of the LMS, and the second and third parts look at the lines of the old Midland Railway, which became the Midland Division of the LMS.

Fortunately, in an historical sense, the structure of the Midland Railway in Birmingham made it comparatively straightforward to divide. The Midland Railway was formed on 10th May 1844 by the amalgamation of the Midland Counties Railway, North Midland Railway and the Birmingham & Derby Junction Railway. In 1844, the Birmingham & Gloucester was an independent railway company with its first Birmingham terminus at Camp Hill, but in 1845 entered into a working agreement with the Bristol & Gloucester Railway whereby the two railways were worked as one, and in 1846 the Bristol & Gloucester amalgamated with the Midland. We therefore decided that Part 2 would concentrate on the former Birmingham & Derby Junction Railway and later lines connecting to it, and Part 3 would cover the former Birmingham & Gloucester Railway and later lines connecting to it.

In order to show the developments that took place, we have used a number of maps and, whilst the Midland Railway distance diagrams largely fulfil our needs, we have included additional sketches of specific stations, etc, and I am very grateful to John Copsey for his help in producing these at short notice.

I am deeply indebted to John Edgington for his very considerable assistance and endorse his remarks that said "It's only right this book should be put together by a couple of Brummies". Although neither of us now live in Birmingham, his opinion is 'once a Brummie, always a Brummie!'. I would also like to thank Mark Norton for his continued confidence in Wild Swan Publications and myself by making his father's work available to enable this book to be produced.

It is inevitable that there will be some duplication of information between the three parts, but we took the view that it would be easier if readers did not have to refer elsewhere for maps of areas where both divisions were operating. We have tried to keep this to a minimum.

I believe these three parts are a unique collection of pictures that provide a wide coverage of the old LMS in the West Midlands, and we should be grateful for D. J. Norton's foresight in taking 'railway' pictures rather than just concentrating upon locomotives or trains.

Finally, I would like to express my thanks to Wynne, for her tolerance during the past few months while I have been locked away in my room working on these books. As she said on more than one occasion, "When am I going to get my husband back?"

Bob Essery

No. 45682 at King's Norton station.

BRICKYARD CROSSING

The short length of line, officially known as the Aston Curve, ran from Duddeston Road to St Andrew's Junction. There were two signal boxes on the line, Landor Street Junction and Brickyard Crossing. Offically this signal box controlled a level crossing, which was an access road to clay pits and a number of brickworks. The first signal box opened before 1876 and the replacement box, seen in this 10th July 1955 picture, was opened on 15th May 1904, closing on 20th February 1966. The line in the background was the old L&NWR route from New Street to Stechford and Coventry. At this point the gradient was 1 in 62, easing to 1 in 85, to where the Camp Hill line crossed over the GWR and all freight trains were banked from Duddeston to either Camp Hill or King's Heath.

5

BIRMINGHAM & GLOUCESTER RAILWAY VIA CAMP HILL

St Andrew's Junction marked the end of the Aston Curve and point where the line from Duddeston, known as the Camp Hill line, connected with the line from Exchange Sidings and Grand Junction. This picture is typical of the Camp Hill line during the early 1950s, a westbound mineral train hauled by an ex-Midland Class 3F 0-6-0, probably banked by another Class 3F. The maximum length of train was equal to 60 wagons and the maximum load for a Class 3F running under Mineral train classification was equal to 40, with a wooden-bodied 13 ton coal wagon being the unit of loading. The guard had to calculate the actual number of wagons and the equivalent loading, for example five empty wagons was equal to two mineral wagons and so on.

While the Birmingham & Derby Junction was building its line from Whitacre to Lawley Street, the Birmingham & Gloucester Railway was approaching Birmingham from the south. In 1840 this line from Gloucester, which included climbing the famous Lickey Incline, was opened to Cofton Farm, and on 17th December to the terminus at Camp Hill. Little is known about this station, which was on what became the main line into Birmingham and was later closed. The second station at Highgate Road dates from c.1864 (the precise date is not recorded) and the goods station is on the up side of the line north of the station. The line was continued towards Curzon Street, and at a point close to where the present-day Grand Junction is situated, a junction, to be known as Gloucester Junction, was made with the London & Birmingham Railway. Thereafter Birmingham & Gloucester passenger trains ran into Curzon Street and Camp Hill remained as a goods depot.

On 10th May 1844, the Birmingham & Derby Junction, Midland Counties, and North Midland Railway amalgamated to form the Midland Railway Company, and less than two years later, on 3rd August 1846, the Birmingham & Gloucester and Bristol & Gloucester, which since 1st July 1845 had

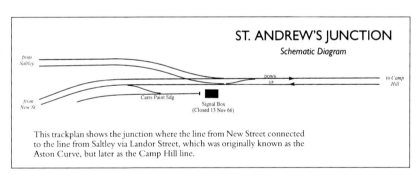

ST. ANDREW'S JUNCTION
Schematic Diagram

from Saltley
from New St.
Carrs Paint Sdg
DOWN
UP
Signal Box
(Closed 13 Nov 66)
to Camp Hill

This trackplan shows the junction where the line from New Street connected to the line from Saltley via Landor Street, which was originally known as the Aston Curve, but later as the Camp Hill line.

been worked as one company, also became part of the Midland Railway.

For a number of years there was no direct route from stations north of Birmingham to destinations to the west. In the section describing the Birmingham West Suburban Railway in Part 2, it was explained that passenger trains from, say, Leeds to Bristol, ran into Birmingham New Street where the train was reversed, with a new locomotive at what had been the end of the train so that it could run via St. Andrew's Junction onto the Camp Hill line. The opening in 1866 of what became known as the Aston Curve, a short length of line from Duddeston to St. Andrew's Junction, transformed traffic movements

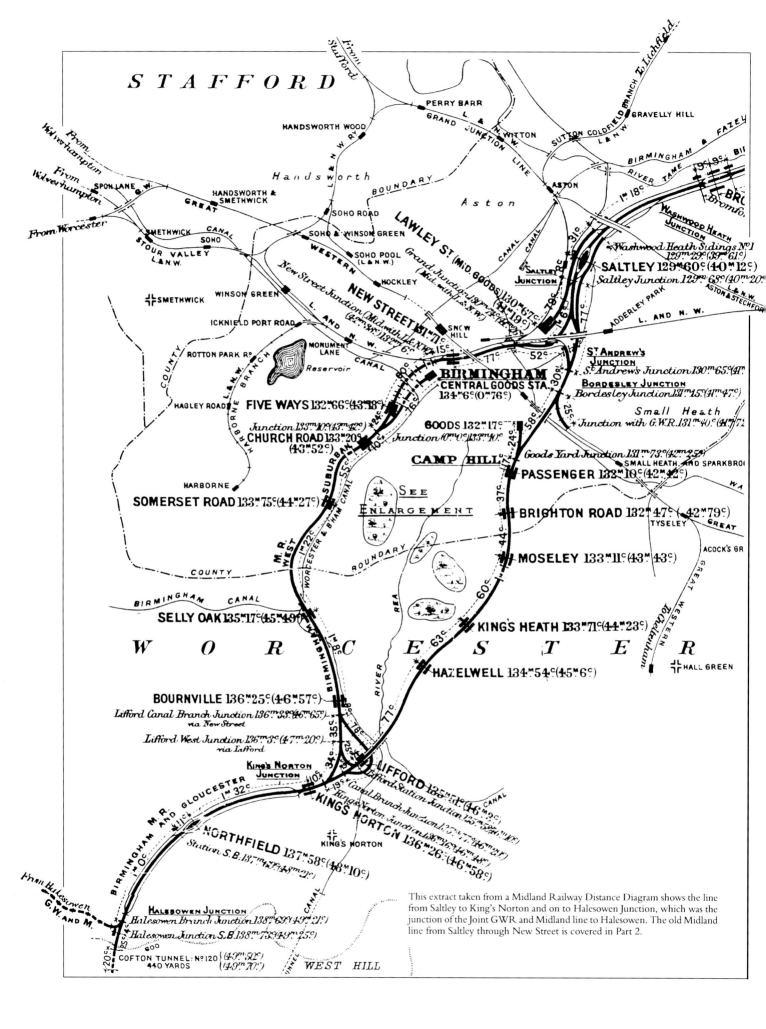

This extract taken from a Midland Railway Distance Diagram shows the line from Saltley to King's Norton and on to Halesowen Junction, which was the junction of the Joint GWR and Midland line to Halesowen. The old Midland line from Saltley through New Street is covered in Part 2.

Although some passenger trains ran over the line between St Andrew's Junction and Grand Junction, they were not commonplace. This picture, taken on Sunday 8th May 1955, shows Class 5X No. 45682 *Trafalgar* with an express passenger train heading for the 'west road.' We should point out that regardless of the precise point of the compass, trains travelling on the down line from Derby towards Bristol were running west or on the west road, but when travelling in the opposite direction, they were described as 'running north.'

from Birmingham along the old Birmingham & Gloucester line to Bristol. Through freight and mineral trains could run along the Camp Hill line and it was also used by a few passenger trains that did not travel via New Street.

Continuing west from St. Andrew's Junction, there was a connection with the GWR at Bordesley; this was used to exchange freight traffic between the GWR (later the Western Region of British Railways) and the Midland (later LMS and finally London Midland Region of British Railways). Between Camp Hill, the first passenger station on the line, and King's Norton, there were also passenger stations at Brighton Road, Moseley, King's Heath, Hazelwell and Lifford. On 27th January 1941, all the stations were closed. This was not due to the loss of traffic, but rather an operational need. When I knew the line in the late 1940s/ early 1950s, the traffic in the up direction was very heavy and it was not unknown for a train to be standing at every stop signal along the line. This was caused by congestion

at Washwood Heath and the knock-on effect could see twenty or so trains in a queue stretching from Washwood Heath to Northfield. The problems of finding a path for a passenger train was immense, so the problem was eased with their removal. However, passenger trains were not entirely eliminated and at least two ran on a daily basis c.1950.

At King's Norton there was a connection with the Birmingham West Suburban Railway and carriage sidings on the down side of the line. There were four running lines between King's Norton and Barnt Green, with a passenger station at Northfield. Before reaching Barnt Green, there was the connection to the Halesowen branch, and at Barnt Green the line divided, the main line continuing towards Bromsgrove with the branch to Redditch and Evesham curving away to the east. Between Barnt Green and Bromsgrove, where our pictorial coverage ends, there was a station at Blackwell and the famous Lickey Incline.

This picture, also taken on Sunday 8th May 1955, shows Saltley's Horwich Mogul No. 42890 at St Andrew's Junction with an express passenger train that had come from somewhere west of Birmingham, heading for New Street. It is possible the train would terminate at Birmingham and the empty stock would be taken to the carriage sidings at King's Norton. If this was the case, then the engine would work the stock to King's Norton over the Birmingham West Suburban line.

This picture was taken from the up line on the Bordesley Junction side of St. Andrew's Junction on 22nd August 1954. The line ahead led to Exchange Sidings and New Street whilst to the right it went past Brickyard Crossing to Landor Street Junction. It was along the section of line behind the photographer that Saltley enginemen were supposed to have made smoke to help Birmingham City football club. Creating a smokescreen was supposed to confuse the opposition, or so the old oft-repeated story goes. Whilst it is true the line runs alongside the 'Blues' football ground, known as St Andrew's, and that black smoke was often a feature of how the engines were being worked along this part of the Camp Hill line, there is no truth in the story that this was done deliberately by the enginemen to help the 'home team'.

This picture was taken from the embankment on the down side of the line, near to St Andrew's Junction on 9th December 1951. The signal box can be seen beyond and below Garrison Lane bridge. This picture also emphasises the industrial nature of this part of Birmingham during the 1950s.

This picture was taken on Sunday 22nd August 1954 from alongside the down Camp Hill line between Bordesley Junction and St Andrew's Junction with Garrison Lane bridge in view. Light engines or trams from the down Camp Hill line that were heading for Exchange Sidings used the crossover. One was No. 38 Trip, which ran between Washwood Heath and Exchange Sidings, did some shunting and then worked traffic to Lawley Street. If the train had 20 or more wagons or the weather was not clear, the train was banked from Duddeston Junction in the normal way, but when the bank engine was over the points the train stopped and, with the bank pilot at the head of the train, it ran into Exchange Sidings with the train engine at the rear. When it was time for the 38 Trip to go to Lawley Street, a Bank Pilot drew the train onto the Camp Hill line and, when the Trip engine was clear of the points, the train reversed. With the Trip engine leading, it ran to Duddeston where 38 Trip was taken across the main lines into Lawley Street and the Bank Pilot ran along the up Camp Hill line to the Bank Pilot siding at Washwood Heath. The signals on the left were for Exchange Sidings, and those on the right were for the Camp Hill line to Brickyard Crossing and Landor Street.

At Bordesley Junction there was a connection with the GWR whose main line from Birmingham to London passed below the Midland line between Bordesley and Camp Hil. The purpose of the line was to allow traffic to be transferred between the Midland, later the LMS, and the GWR and after 1948 between London Midland Region and Western Region of British Railways. Most of the traffic was coal for the GWR and empty wagons being returned to the collieries. During the postwar period, there was also a considerable traffic in motor vehicle chassis and parts that came from Oxford to destinations in Birmingham. To handle this traffic, five trip engines, Trip Nos 22, 23, 24, 25 and 26, were engaged upon this work. The locomotives were manned throughout the 24 hours from Monday until Sunday morning when the Saturday night shift brought the last one back to Saltley shed. The usual locomotive booked for this work was a Class 8F 2-8-0 and Class 4F 0-6-0, but the usual practice was to allocate engines that were approaching the time they went into the shops for repairs, so it was not unusual to see a Horwich Mogul or Class 5 on the 'Bordesley trippers' as they were known by local railwaymen. This picture, looking towards Camp Hill, was taken on Sunday 22nd August 1954. The line to the left was the start of the branch to the GWR, which was built as a single line but doubled on 13th July 1941.

Class 4F No. 43965 from 17B Burton heading a semi-fitted, as railwaymen would describe it, past Bordesley Junction signal box on Wednesday 4th August 1954. The train was probably a Burton to Gloucester working and the term 'semi fitted' meant that at least one third of the wagons were fitted with an automatic vacuum brake connected to the locomotive. The large building above and behind the locomotive was the Birmingham Corporation Coventry Road garage for trolley buses which worked the city centre route to Yardley and Sheldon. Within a few years they had been replaced by buses.

BORDESLEY JUNCTION

This view provides a clear view of Bordesley Junction signal box, which was opened on 6th April 1941. The connection between the GWR and the Midland was opened as a single line on 1st November 1861, but I am not certain how the line was worked. In 1909 it is recorded that the method was as a single line worked by a staff without tickets, and in 1928 electric key token working replaced a pilot guard, which presumably replaced the method used for a period prior to 1928. In order to cope with the increase of traffic during the Second World War, the line was doubled and double track working began on 13th July 1941. The final change came about March 1967 when absolute block working began. This was required to permit the increased passenger services that followed electrification in the Birmingham area to run over the line.

This picture of the interior of Bordesley Junction signal box on 31st March 1954 gives some idea of what the inside was like during the hours of darkness. Before leaving Bordesley, we should explain that the Bordesley Trips were banked and the train ran forward to stand at the GWR signal to await permission to run into the GWR sidings. However, as soon as possible, the bank engine was reversed and ran over the crossover, onto the up Camp Hill line in order to return to Washwood Heath for its next banking duty. Finally, note that on the extreme right there appears to be LNWR permissive block instruments.

After crossing the old GWR Birmingham to London line at Bordesley, but before arriving at Camp Hill, a down train running on the old Midland line would cross over the Warwick & Birmingham Canal. This picture was taken on 10th July 1955 looking in a southerly direction towards Small Heath. Between the GWR station at Small Heath and Bordesley, the GWR had extensive sidings on both sides of the line; it was also the point where there was a considerable exchange of traffic between both companies, beginning with the GWR and Midland, then the GWR and LMS, and finally between the London Midland and Western Regions of British Railways. On the far left of the picture, part of the GWR down sidings can be seen.

This road underbridge (the road passes under the railway) was over the A34 Birmingham to Stratford Road. This picture, taken on Sunday 20th March 1955, was looking towards the city centre, with the line from Bordesley Junction to the right and Camp Hill station to the left. Beyond the bridge, the road climbed to a point where Stratford Street, Stratford Place and Stratford Road come together; this is known as Camp Hill, which gave the district its name. At this point the Camp Hill line was still climbing, but the gradient had eased to 1 in 280.

Taken during the early evening of 4th July 1953, the final day of tram operation in Birmingham, tram 703 was one of a group being transferred across the city to Kyotts Lake Road depot where it would be scrapped. Passing the Shakespeare public house on the Stratford Road, with the turret belonging to King Edward's Camp Hill School in the background, the railway bridge carries the Camp Hill line from Bordesley Junction to Camp Hill.

CAMP HILL

The passenger station at Camp Hill closed on 27th January 1941 but the large goods station, seen in this 22nd August 1954 picture, remained open until 7th February 1966 when it was also closed. The large building, which can been seen in other pictures of Camp Hill, was the goods and grain warehouse. Although the goods station at Camp Hill was smaller than Lawley Street and Birmingham Central, it handled a fair amount of traffic, in particular agricultural produce for the City's markets. There was a small coal wharf at Highgate Road, which was on the Brighton Road side of the station. There was, as far as I recall, one shunt engine at the depot. About 1948 it was a Class 1F 0-6-0T, but later a Diesel shunter was employed. Arriving on a Monday morning, it remained at Camp Hill for the entire week and was manned by men who were out-stationed at Camp Hill.

This c1953 picture is one of a pair showing freight trains heading west along the Camp Hill line and appears to have been taken from the signal box. Class 4F No. 44516 was hauling a stopping freight train which was the first part of a double freight train. Overleaf we show the rear train that was coupled to the leading train.

This is a remarkable picture and one that requires some explanation. The train was on the down Camp Hill line passing Camp Hill signal box. The Class 3F 0-6-0 was hauling a train but it was also coupled to the brakevan of the train in front. There were a number of places where it was permitted to couple two trains together so that you had, train engine, train, brakevan, train engine, train, brakevan and, on the Camp Hill line, a bank engine. In the Birmingham area this formation was permitted on the main line between Landor Street Junction and Lifford Station Junction or King's Norton station, and on the goods line between Water Orton station junction and Landor Street junction, and also between Saltley Junction and Water Orton junction. From an operating standpoint, to use a railwayman's expression, it 'saved a block'; in other words two trains passing through a section as one train saved time when there was a lot of traffic building up. It was a spectacular sight but rarely photographed.

Class 3F 0-6-0 No. 43464 heading west with a Class H Through freight train past Camp Hill signal box c1953. This was the third signal box at Camp Hill and it was opened on 23rd February 1941. Banking westbound freight trains usually ceased at Camp Hill, but if the driver of the train engine required further assistance, he would whistle as he passed the box and in daylight the signalman would wave his arm to tell the bank pilot driver to continue to King's Heath; if it was dark, then he would wave a green lamp.

Parallel-boiler 2-6-4T No. 42337 approaching Camp Hill with an Ordinary passenger train on Sunday 8th May 1955. At this time there were very few passenger trains running over the Camp Hill line – they were in the way of the very heavy freight traffic that was heading for Birmingham's marshalling yards!

With the remains of Camp Hill station to the left and the outline of the goods and grain warehouse in the far distance, this was the view to be seen by enginemen on an up train. Note the water crane at the end of the platform with Montpelier Street underline bridge beyond. Photographed on Sunday 18th July 1954.

BRIGHTON ROAD

The Up Outer Home for Camp Hill photographed on 19th April 1954 Although the original Midland post had been retained, an LMS upper quadrant arm had replaced the Midland lower quadrant arm.

The station at Brighton Road, opened on 1st November 1875, was closed on 27th January 1941, together with the other passenger stations on the Camp Hill line. A few months later, on 4th May 1941, the signal box was closed and colour light IBS signals were installed. This picture was taken on 19th April 1954 and shows the site of the station.

This shows the site of Moseley station, which was opened on 1st November 1867 and closed on 27th January 1941. The locomotive, Saltley 21A Class 4F No. 44150, was heading a westbound Class K Stopping freight train that was about to enter Moseley tunnel.

MOSELEY

Dogpool lane on the outskirts of Moseley, February 1954, at the point where it crosses the River Rea. As the road bears to the right close to the Highbury public house, it becomes Dads Lane, and D. J. Norton's father, Arthur, ran a greengrocers store here for many years. Where Dads Lane becomes Avenue Road, the Camp Hill line from King's Heath to Hazelwell passes overhead.

Moseley tunnel had a rather distinctive shape, which makes this a somewhat artistic picture taken on 19th April 1954. This shows the site of the passenger station – there were no goods facilities at Moseley. It was built in a cutting and, with King's Heath less than a mile away, there was no need. The rather imposing bridge carries Wood Bridge Road, so named because the first bridge was made of wood.

The distinctive shape of the mouth of Moseley tunnel is seen in this picture taken from the down line 'four-foot', facing west towards King's Heath station on 7th February 1954. The Ballast Sidings were to the right of the picture, and although not visible in this view, they can be seen on the opposite page. Note the distinctive shape of the Brighton Road 1B signal, which is also featured in the following picture.

This picture of 21A Saltley's Class 4F No. 44211 with an empty coaching stock train was taken on Easter Monday, 19th April 1954. The train was moving on the up line passing Leighton Road, which was at the top of the bank. The signal was the Brighton Road up I.B distant for Camp Hill.

The ballast sidings at King's Heath were on the up side of the line between King's Heath station and the west end of Moseley tunnel, which can be seen in the distance. They were only used by the engineering dept and the level of activity varied.

One of Saltley's Class 3Fs heading west with a Class H Through freight train. There was a lot of steam leaking from the front end and this was not welcomed by enginemen.

Class 4F No. 44553 from 22A Bristol heading a westbound mineral train, probably a Washwood Heath to Westerleigh working, approaching King's Heath station on 31st March 1954.

Through the bridge to the left we can see the lines leading to the ballast sidings and on the right the siding was described on the LMS sidestrip diagram as Ellis Coal Wharf with a holding capacity of 12 wagons. King's Heath was as far as the bank pilots went and the crossover and ground signals to enable them to return to Washwood Heath can be seen below the bridge.

KING'S HEATH

We continue the survey of King's Heath with this picture of a Class 5 No. 44736 on an up express running through on Thursday 16th August 1952. It is not possible to say if the train was using the Camp Hill line to bypass New Street, an excursion train from the west to a destination north of Birmingham, or if for operational reasons it was to enter the station from the Derby end in order to depart over the Birmingham West Suburban line. If it was the latter, the train would have terminated at New Street and run as empty stock to the carriage sidings at King's Norton.

A typical mid-1950s scene at King's Heath with 22A Bristol Class 4F No. 44087 hauling a Class H Through freight train which appears to have been made up of empty mineral wagons, probably heading for Washwood Heath up sidings. Note the composition of the train; at this date (the picture was taken on 18th September 1955) 16 ton steel mineral wagons were being built to replace the older 13 ton wooden-body wagons, so a mixture of both types would be found in mineral wagon trains.

King's Heath station, looking west towards King's Norton, with the goods yard to the left behind the station building. When this picture was taken on 13th June 1957, the passenger station had been closed since 1941 but the goods station was to remain open until it was closed on 2nd May 1966.

This picture was also taken looking towards King's Norton but from the forecourt on 6th August 1958. It shows the road approach and the goods yard beyond.

Class 8F No. 48635 heading west through King's Heath with a Mineral, probably bound for Westerleigh with traffic for the west of England.

This winter's scene, taken on 12th January 1959, shows Class 3F No. 43223 hauling a Class H Through freight train on the up line at King's Heath. By 1959 the number of Class 3Fs in service was declining, but a few years were to elapse before the class became extinct. I have always thought they were splendid engines and, unlike the Class 4S, which could vary as far as steaming qualities were concerned, there was virtually no such thing as a poor-steaming Class 3F.

The importance of this picture, taken on 27th January 1952, is that it shows a bank pilot engine in the 'pilot siding' waiting to return to Washwood Heath. Generally the practice was to send the pilots back as soon as there was a path, but when this was not possible they stood in the short siding. When this happened, it was not unknown for the driver to have a word with the signalman to see if there was enough time for him to go to the pub for a pint, leaving his fireman in charge of the engine!

King's Heath station from the west end looking towards Camp Hill. The station was renamed from Moseley on 1st November 1867 when the station at Moseley was opened.

During the 1950s the surviving Class 2Fs in the Birmingham area were employed on some of the local trip workings. This picture, taken during 1953, shows No. 58143 running tender first towards Camp Hill with what appears to have been a local trip working, although the first wagon suggests that it may have been heading for the ballast sidings to the north of King's Heath station, as shown at page 25.

There were five sidings at King's Heath which could be used for traffic purposes and a private siding belonging to the Birmingham Corporation. There was also a trailing connection from the up line, as seen here, and a short shunting neck together with a trailing connection from the down line. Signalling plans show a ground frame controlled the down connection to the sidings, which appear to have been little used in the final years before the goods facilities were withdrawn on 1st March 1965. This picture was taken on 14th March 1962.

This appears to be an example of a Midland Railway 5 ton portable hand crane photographed on 8th June 1955. Cranes of this type (the Midland also had a 4 ton version) were taken to stations when the existing crane was unable to lift a load. With the work completed, the crane would then be moved elsewhere.

HAZELWELL

Hazelwell was the next station along the line after King's Heath. It opened for passenger and goods traffic on 1st January 1903. There were six sidings in the yard with a capacity to hold 66 wagons and two lay-bys, one for traffic in each direction, both long enough to hold 44 wagons. This overall view of the station was taken on 26th March 1950 looking towards King's Heath.

The extent of the platform awnings is emphasised in this picture, taken on 26th March 1950, looking west towards King's Norton. The signal box and goods sidings were the other side of the roadbridge.

Hazelwell station entrance, photographed on 27th August 1961, was on the Cartland Road which ran over the railway and, as can be seen in the previous picture, passengers used the inclined path to reach the platforms.

Hazelwell signal box was opened on 6th April 1902, but the date of closure is uncertain; one source gives 7th September 1969. The connection seen on the left-hand side of the picture was to the up lay-by. The short blind siding was long enough to hold a wagon, and at times it would have been used to supply the signalman with coal for his stove. The train hauled by Class 4F No. 44411 was a Class E 'Maltese', an express freight train where the four leading vehicles were equipped with automatic vacuum brakes that were coupled to the engine to increase the braking power available to the driver. This allowed the train to run faster than an express freight train where there was no additional brake power available.

This picture shows the down lay-by at Hazelwell on 12th September 1954. The traffic sidings at this station were on the Kings' Norton side of the station; the lay-by was at the opposite end of the station. Opposite we show a train setting back onto the lay-by which, to the best of my knowledge at this period, was used for storage purposes rather than by through trains that were 'put inside' so that a following train could pass.

The 'Austerities' were not commonplace on the Midland Division in the Birmingham area, but, as we can see from this picture taken on 17th January 1954, they were not unknown. No.90102 was stationed at 26B Agecroft, but why a Central Division engine was at Hazelwell is unclear.

There was a down lay-by on the King's Heath side of Hazelwell station and this picture, taken on 17 January 1954, shows Class 5 No. 44917 setting back; note the ground signal in the clear position. The lay-by would hold 44 wagons and, whilst it is difficult to be sure, it is possible the brakevan had been left on the running line and some wagons were being set back for storage on the lay-by. There appears to be more than 44 wagons in the train.

British Railways Class 9F No. 92046 from 18A Toton heading an up train of empty mineral wagons running under Class J headlamp code. The train had just passed through Hazelwell station and was passing the down lay-by, which can be seen on the left of the picture.

Tender-first working on local trip turns was commonplace in the Birmingham area and whilst we cannot identify which trip working this was, we can say the train was being hauled by Class 3F No. 43523 and was running on the up line approaching Pineapple bridge. The picture was taken on 4th March 1956.

Class 3F No.43223 passing below Fordhouse Lane bridge with a down Class K stopping freight train of what appears to have been empty mineral wagons.

Part of the line between Hazelwell and Lifford was on an embankment and included a bridge over the Worcester & Birmingham canal, seen in this picture. The locomotive was another of 21A Saltley's Class 4Fs, No. 43941, hauling a Class K Stopping freight train, and photographed on 4th March 1956.

LIFFORD

This picture of Lifford Station Junction was taken on 26th July 1954 when D.J.Norton was in the signal box. The view is facing north towards Landor Street Junction and the lines curving away to the left go to Lifford West Junction where they connect with the Birmingham West Suburban Railway. Goods trains from the north heading for Birmingham Central Goods Station went over this route in order to avoid passing through New Street station and reversing at Church Road Junction. We have covered this line in Part 2. To the left we can see the goods yard close to the site of the passenger station which was closed on 27th January 1941.

Tram No. 840 tackling Breedon Hill on the route from Stirchley to Cotteridge in March 1952. Just to the left of the tram is the Breedon Cross Hotel, which used to stand on the corner of Lifford Lane.

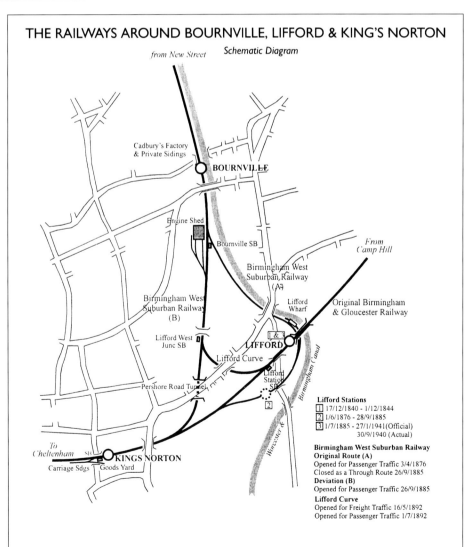

THE RAILWAYS AROUND BOURNVILLE, LIFFORD & KING'S NORTON

Schematic Diagram

from New Street

Cadbury's Factory & Private Sidings

BOURNVILLE

Engine Shed

Bournville SB

Birmingham West Suburban Railway (A)

From Camp Hill

Birmingham West Suburban Railway (B)

Lifford Wharf

Original Birmingham & Gloucester Railway

Lifford West Junc SB

1 & 3

LIFFORD

Lifford Curve

Birmingham Canal

Lifford Station SB

Pershore Road Tunnel

2

To Cheltenham SB

KINGS NORTON

Worcester &

Carriage Sdgs   Goods Yard

Lifford Stations
1 17/12/1840 - 1/12/1844
2 1/6/1876 - 28/9/1885
3 1/7/1885 - 27/1/1941(Official)
     30/9/1940 (Actual)

Birmingham West Suburban Railway
Original Route (A)
Opened for Passenger Traffic 3/4/1876
Closed as a Through Route 26/9/1885
Deviation (B)
Opened for Passenger Traffic 26/9/1885
Lifford Curve
Opened for Freight Traffic 16/5/1892
Opened for Passenger Traffic 1/7/1892

The changes that took place at Lifford were complex and are shown in the accompanying diagram. Between 1840 and 1940 there were three stations at Lifford, all on different sites. We included some pictures of the canal branch in Part 2 when describing the Birmingham West Suburban Railway but here we have tried to cover as many aspects as possible using D.J.Norton's pictures. The second station at Lifford is shown on page 49.

The third station at Lifford was closed for passenger traffic on 30th September 1940 and this picture, taken on 7th March 1950, shows Class 3F No. 43812 from 21A Saltley heading a westbound Class J Mineral train close to the site of the old station. Note the goods sidings on the up side of the line.

This rather ornate building, Lifford station's goods shed, was situated by bridge 134. Note the bridge plate which was probably the old Birmingham & Gloucester number from Gloucester.

This end view of the old goods shed shows the bricked-up rail entrance to the shed, and confirms that the rails had been lifted, and illustrates a modern feature, a bicycle shed for employees.

Lifford Station Junction looking towards King's Norton on 29th July 1957. The old Birmingham & Gloucester line, with Lifford Station Junction signal box visible, is straight ahead, with the Lifford curve to the Birmingham & West Suburban line to the right. The connection to the sidings and shunting neck can also be seen on the right of the picture.

As we can see from this 3rd May 1953 picture, Lifford Station Junction Signal Box was opposite the junction of the Lifford Curve where it joined the Camp Hill line; it is just visible beyond the embankment to the left of the picture. We can also see the checkrails on the inside curve. The down line was from Camp Hill through the junction, but when the line reached Lifford West Junction it became the up line to Bournville and beyond. The reverse applied to down trains from the Birmingham West Suburban line; at Lifford West Junction they became up trains and continued to run on the up Camp Hill line as they ran towards Landor Street Junction.

The Lifford curve was a facing connection between the Birmingham & Gloucester line to Camp Hill and the Birmingham West Suburban line from New Street to King's Norton. This short length of railway came into use on 16th May and was opened for passenger traffic on 1st July 1892. It was closed for regular passenger traffic on 27th January 1941 but reopened on 6th March 1967. Although a tight curve, part of it had a checkrail. It was a very useful connection for operating purposes.

This later picture, taken on 18th February 1961, also illustrates Lifford Station Junction looking towards King's Norton. The old Birmingham & Gloucester line with Lifford Station Junction signal box visible is seen straight ahead, with the Lifford curve to the Birmingham & West Suburban line to the right. Note the new factory building which had been built since the previous picture was taken in 1957 and shown at page 44.

It was not possible to run from the goods sidings at Lifford onto the down Birmingham & Gloucester without first running onto the up main line, then crossing to the down line over the trailing crossover by the signal box. This picture, taken on 18th February 1961, shows Class 2F No. 58138 with a trip working leaving the sidings at Lifford. It would also be possible to run into the sidings from the down line; the disc signal by the crossover would allow a train to run onto the up main line, then it could draw forward onto the loop, which was connected to the head shunt with the engine the correct end of the train to shunt the sidings.

This interior view of Lifford Station Junction signal box was taken during the hours of darkness on 28th September 1959, when D.J. Norton was visiting friendly signalmen.

On 10th June 1963 this picture was taken at the junction of the canal branch, facing towards King's Norton. GWR Hall Class No. 5984 *Linden Hall* is seen here with a class D semi-fitted express freight train. Based upon pictorial evidence, some GWR locomotives worked through to Exchange Sidings.

This picture shows the junction of the canal branch with the Birmingham & Gloucester line between Lifford and King's Norton. In the distance we can see Lifford Station Junction signal box, which should help readers identify the position of the junction. Note the ground frame which was bolt locked by Lifford Station Junction signal box. This ground frame controlled train movements at this end of the canal branch.

The second station at Lifford was on the Birmingham West Suburban line and opened on 1st June 1876, but closed when the third station was opened on 28th September 1885. This picture was taken during 1953 and shows the disused station and siding that were not in use.

This picture of Lifford Canal sidings was taken on 10th June 1963 from where the old Birmingham & Gloucester Railway crosses the Worcester & Birmingham Canal, which can be seen to the right. The arrangement of the sidings corresponds with what is shown on the 1904 Ordnance Survey map, but when the picture was taken, there was an air of neglect; the days of canal and railway interchange had ceased at Lifford.

This view was taken on the canal branch from below Pershore Road bridge. The embankment carries the old Birmingham & Gloucester Railway. Lifford station and the Worcester and Birmingham Canal were to the right but not visible in this 12th September 1954 picture.

The old canal bridge over the Worcester–Birmingham Canal on Lifford Lane, near the junction with Melchett Road, in March 1962. The big chimney marks the site of the R. J. Hunt iron foundry. The construction of a more functional modern bridge was brought about after the creation of a refuse works off Ebury Road. Many large lorries crossed this bridge daily and the narrow old bridge would surely have suffered. Further down Lifford Lane, the Stratford-upon-Avon Canal is also crossed. Here the old bridge does survive and the road narrows markedly.

We begin our extended photographic coverage of King's Norton with this picture of Class 4F No. 44450 approaching King's Norton on the down line from the Birmingham West Suburban Railway on 12th February 1961. Some people are seen in one of the wagons of this short ballast train.

This picture of Class 5X No. 45572 *Eire* heading a westbound express for Bristol on 15th May 1955 was taken from the other side of the line, facing the embankment from where the previous picture was taken. The train was about to enter King's Norton station from the Birmingham West Suburban line, with the Camp Hill line in the foreground.

Taken from the centre of Pershore Road South during April 1963, this picture was looking towards the centre of Cotteridge village. The railway line to King's Norton passes under the road at this point. On the far left the sign for King's Norton Station can be seen and Cotteridge fire station is visible on the right.

KING'S NORTON

King's Norton was both an important and interesting place. It was the junction of the old Birmingham & Gloucester's line into Birmingham, known as the Camp Hill line, and the later Birmingham West Suburban Railway, which, after doubling and some realigning plus the extension from Church Road Junction to New Street, provided a more direct and faster route into New Street station. It was also where the down goods line began and the up goods line ceased. There were a number of sidings on the down side of the line. The goods sidings for local traffic could hold 90 wagons and the facilities included a goods shed. There were some sidings allocated to the Engineer's Dept and a connection to the private sidings owned by the Triplex Safety Glass Co. Finally, there were the carriage sidings, which, in conjunction with the carriage sidings at Saltley, provided the storage and servicing facilities for all passenger stock based on the Midland Division in the Birmingham area.

Standard Class 4F 0-6-0s are normally associated with freight trains but at times they could be found on both Ordinary passenger trains and excursion trains, often running under express passenger train headlamp code. This picture, taken on 19th September 1955, shows No. 44002 from 19C Canklow at the head of an Ordinary passenger train. Why and how a 19C engine came to be working this train is unclear.

The locomotives stationed at Bournville were largely employed on passenger work but they also covered a number of local trip workings on the south-west side of Birmingham. Class 3F No. 43521 was one of the freight engines stationed at 21B when it was photographed at King's Norton on 28th December 1954.

This overall view of King's Norton station was taken on 17th February 1957, facing west towards Bromsgrove from the down Camp Hill line platform, with the island platform in the centre and West Suburban side of the station clearly visible on the right side of the picture.

The original station at King's Norton was opened on 1st May 1849 but we are unsure when this building, which was on the down Camp Hill line platform, was built. There were four platform faces at King's Norton, separate up and down platforms for the Camp Hill and Birmingham West Suburban lines. As we can see, the up Camp Hill and down West Suburban were opposite sides of an island platform.

The presence of two ex–GWR Brakevans hauled by an unidentified 0-6-0 in this c1953 picture is not easy to explain but it may have been part of an engineers train that was working in the area.

This picture was taken from the west end of the West Suburban lines and shows, on the left, the up platform and on the right the down platform. King's Norton station was rebuilt with extra platforms and junctions which came into use on 14th March 1926.

During the earlier period when D.J.Norton was taking pictures, it was not uncommon to find some of the local passenger services were worked by Class 2P 4-4-0s. This picture, taken on 26th April 1953, shows No. 40426 from 22A Bristol with a down Ordinary passenger train at King's Norton.

Class F express freight train hauled by Class 3F No. 43673 photographed c1953. When the picture was taken, the end of the train was still on the up goods line and across both the up and down main lines, with the engine just on the up Camp Hill line. Because this involved blocking both the up and down main lines at busy times, goods train were often held for some time on the goods lines before they were allowed to run onto Camp Hill line.

Class 5 No. 44691 hauling a Class E express freight train from the up main onto the up Camp Hill line on 5th May 1962. The side of the goods shed can be seen on the left of the picture and the coaches seen on the right were on the up goods line.

This picture evokes memories. About two and a half years earlier, Fireman Essery came from King's Norton carriage sidings with a similar train of empty coaches heading for New Street where the stock would form a Saturday special to Sheffield. This picture was taken on 4th September 1953 and shows Class 5 No. 44845 from 26G Belle Vue carrying a M826 special train reporting board.

This picture was taken on 9th May 1954 from the footbridge and shows the track layout to the west or Bromsgrove side of the station, with to the left the small dock and the timber goods shed beyond. The two running lines on the left were the down and up Camp Hill lines that joined with the main lines. Opposite the signal box, seen in the centre of the picture, we have from left to right, down goods and down main, up main and up goods lines. Note the pointwork almost opposite the signal box that enabled a train to run from the up goods onto the up Camp Hill line, but any train on the up goods that had to run onto the West Suburban line continued on the up goods to the stop signal on a short post seen at the right of the picture. Finally, note the line running from the West Suburban line into the sidings; this was the departure line for empty carriage stock trains running into New Street.

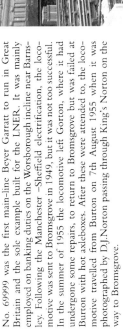

In this picture we can see the other side of the timber goods shed, which can also be seen in the picture above. In the distance, King's Norton station, with the footbridge where the photographer was standing when the previous view was taken, is clearly visible. Although there were some sidings at King's Norton to deal with local traffic, its most important feature were the carriages sidings that can be seen in some of the views. However, we must not overlook that at this time when traffic was heavy, some westbound freight trains started from King's Norton rather than Washwood Heath and a few sidings were used to marshal the wagons into train order. To the best of my recollection, it was mostly mineral traffic for Westerleigh near Bristol.

No. 69999 was the first main-line Beyer Garratt to run in Great Britain and the sole example built for the LNER. It was mainly employed on banking duties on the Worsborough incline near Barnsley. Following the Manchester–Sheffield electrification, the locomotive was sent to Bromsgrove in 1949, but it was not too successful. In the summer of 1955 the locomotive left Gorton, where it had undergone some repairs, to return to Bromsgrove but was failed at Burton with hot axleboxes. After these were attended to, the locomotive travelled from Burton on 7th August 1955 when it was photographed by D.J.Norton passing through King's Norton on the way to Bromsgrove.

Photographed from a signal post on 10th January 1959, this picture shows King's Norton signal box which was on the west side of the station; the bridge connecting the platforms can be seen in the distance. The running line in front of the signal box was the down goods line and the others were the down and up main lines. The coaches were standing on the up goods line; it was not uncommon to store coaches at the end of the goods line. The connection from the goods line to the up main line was behind the photographer, but the crossover to allow trains to run from the up goods line to the up Camp Hill and the down Camp Hill to the down main line can be seen in the centre of the picture.

In many ways this picture is typical of the scene at King's Norton during the early 1950s. Class 4F No. 44248 from 21A Saltley heading west along the down goods line with a mineral train which almost certainly started from Washwood Heath. The picture was taken from the signal box on 24th January 1954.

This winter's scene shows Class 4MT No. 43047 with an Ordinary passenger train passing King's Norton signal box with what was almost certainly a Birmingham New Street to Ashchurch via Evesham train on 10th January 1959.

Photographed from King's Norton signal box on 7th March 1954, we see Class 5 No. 44945 from 17A Derby on an express passenger train for Bristol. The up goods line is seen to the left of the picture, then the up main line; the train was on the down main line. The two running lines between the train and the signal box were the up and down Camp Hill line.

This picture was taken on 20th July 1958 and illustrates a special train passing King's Norton signal box, conveying army tanks hauled by Class 4F No. 44171 along the down goods line, possibly under the lowest category of 'out of gauge' loads.

This picture, taken from King's Norton signal box on 21st November 1955, shows Class 4MT 2-6-4T No. 42054, a Saltley 21A engine, departing from the carriage sidings with an empty stock train. The sidings to the left were used for storing coaches, and the grounded coach body was probably used by the carriage cleaning staff and the vans to hold stores. The signal on the right of the picture was for the down goods line.

By 8th July 1956 the diesels were working many passenger trains in the Birmingham area. This view shows a diesel excursion train comprising three two-car sets of original Derby lightweight stock from Birmingham New Street to Malvern shortly after it had departed from King's Norton.

This overall view of King's Norton was looking north towards Birmingham, with to the left, the up goods line and the connection that enabled trains to run onto the up Camp Hill line. However, note the extension which only connected to the West Suburban line; this was often used to store carriages.

This is another picture taken from a signal post. To the left we can see the up goods line occupied by a goods train, then the up and down main lines. The scissors crossover connected the down goods line with one of the lines that formed part of the sidings, whilst to the right we see the carriage sidings.

NORTHFIELD

The first station at Northfield was opened on 1st September 1870 and a replacement was brought into use during the first months of 1893. The new station was an island platform on an embankment, with the goods lines outside of the up and down main lines. The goods lines ran from Halesowen Junction to King's Norton and were opened between King's Norton and Northfield on 1st May 1892 and between Northfield and Halesowen Junction during 1894. The final change came in 1978 when on 23rd April the goods lines were made slow lines and on 8th May when the outside platform came into use. This picture, looking towards King's Norton on 8th August 1954, shows Class 2F No. 58143 from 21B Bournville shed standing on the down line with a relaying train. As we can see, the down goods line had been lifted prior to relaying. There were three goods siding on the up side of the line which can be seen on the left side of the picture.

The goods sidings at Northfield were on the up side of the line although when this picture was taken in 1953 they do not appear to have been very busy. Class 8F No. 48121 was running as a light engine on the up goods line.

This winter's scene, photographed on 27th February 1955, shows the station with its island platform and station buildings with their awning. The wagons on the left of the picture were in the sidings and the Class 4F No. 44590 was hauling a down Class J mineral train.

This is a similar view to the previous picture but taken in 1953. The locomotive, another Class 4F No. 44179, was hauling a westbound Class H Through freight train.

Northfield station was on an embankment and passengers arriving at the station entrance on West Heath Road had a number of steps to climb in order to reach the platform.

Cast-iron notice boards survived for many years and it was commonplace to find the notice boards of the pregroup companies in place during the British Railways period. However, after 1948 when a replacement was required, a British Transport Commission board was installed. This picture was taken at Northfield on 16th May 1955.

Class 3F No. 43381 from 21A Saltley hauling a Class J mineral train along the down goods line. The signal box, seen in this picture, was at the Bromsgrove end of the station. The right arm of the bracket signals was for the goods line to Halesowen Junction and the other arm was reversed if a down train on the goods line was to be turned out main line.

This picture was taken from the gallery of the up goods line home bracket signal, looking towards King's Norton, with Northfield station visible in the centre of the picture, on 20th June 1954. The line running across the picture from the bottom right-hand corner towards the left top was a trailing connection that allowed a locomotive (and wagons) to run from the down goods or main line onto the up main or goods line, or into the sidings on the up side of the station.

A view of Northfield, looking towards Birmingham from the junction of the Bristol Road South and Rochester Road, in October 1962. As the main road to Bristol grew in importance, the growth of the village saw the centre move away from St Lawrence's Church and the site of Northfield Railway Station.

Midland signals remained in service into the British Railways period and this view of the up home signals at Northfield illustrates this point. The up main line signal was an LMS tubular-post upper quadrant signal, but the up goods line signals were mounted on an original Midland wooden bracket with lower quadrant arms. The left-hand arm was to continue along the up goods line and the right-hand arm was lowered when the train was to be turned out onto the up main line.

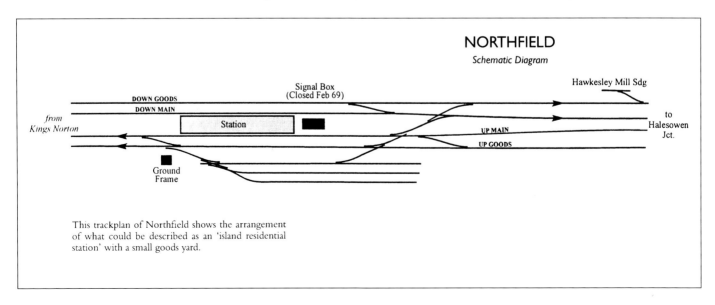

This trackplan of Northfield shows the arrangement of what could be described as an 'island residential station' with a small goods yard.

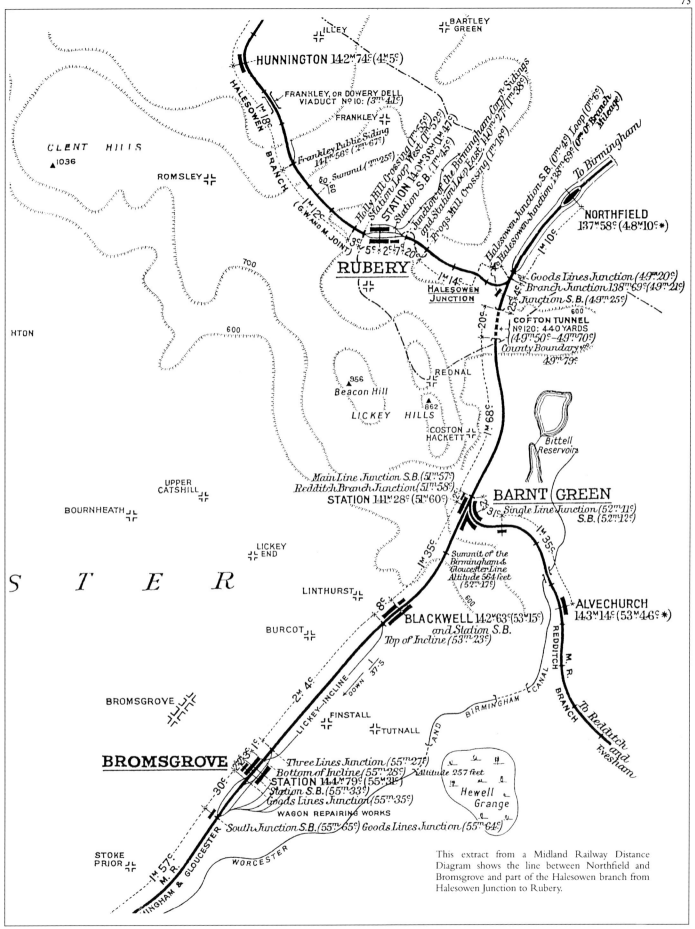

CLENT HILLS
▲1036

ILLEY

BARTLEY GREEN

HUNNINGTON 142ᵐ74ᶜ (4ᵐ5ᶜ)

FRANKLEY, OR DOWERY DELL
VIADUCT Nº 10. (3ᵐ41ᶜ)

FRANKLEY

ROMSLEY

Frankley Public Siding
117ᵐ56ᶜ (2ᵐ67ᶜ)

Summit (7ᵐ25ᶜ)

Holly Hill Crossing (7ᵐ35ᶜ)
Station Loop West (7ᵐ52ᶜ)
Station S.B. 140ᵐ36ᶜ (7ᵐ45ᶜ)
Junction of the Birmingham Corp. Sidings
and Station Loop East 140ᵐ27ᶜ (7ᵐ38ᶜ)
Frog's Mill Crossing (7ᵐ18ᶜ)

Halesowen Junction S.B. (0ᵐ4ᶜ) Loop (0ᵐ6ᶜ)
Halesowen Junction 138ᵐ69ᶜ (0ᵐ0ᶜ Branch Mileage)
to Halesowen Junction

To Birmingham

NORTHFIELD
137ᵐ58ᶜ (4.8ᵐ10ᶜ＊)

RUBERY

HALESOWEN JUNCTION

Goods Lines Junction (4.9ᵐ20ᶜ)
Branch Junction 138ᵐ69ᶜ (4.9ᵐ21ᶜ)
Junction S.B. (4.9ᵐ25ᶜ)

COFTON TUNNEL
Nº 120: 440 YARDS
(4.9ᵐ50ᶜ–4.9ᵐ70ᶜ)
County Boundary
4.9ᵐ79ᶜ

HTON

700

600

REDNAL

Beacon Hill
▲956

LICKEY HILLS

▲862
COSTON
HACKETT

Bittell
Reservoir

UPPER CATSHILL

Main Line Junction S.B. (51ᵐ57ᶜ)
Redditch Branch Junction (51ᵐ58ᶜ)
STATION 141ᵐ28ᶜ (51ᵐ60ᶜ)

BARNT GREEN

BOURNHEATH

Single Line Junction (52ᵐ11ᶜ)
S.B. (52ᵐ12ᶜ)

LICKEY END

Summit of the
Birmingham &
Gloucester Line
Altitude 564 feet
(52ᵐ17ᶜ)

ALVECHURCH
143ᵐ14ᶜ (53ᵐ46ᶜ＊)

STER

LINTHURST

BLACKWELL 142ᵐ63ᶜ (53ᵐ15ᶜ)
and Station S.B.
Top of Incline (53ᵐ23ᶜ)

BURCOT

LICKEY INCLINE
DOWN 1 37.5

REDDITCH BRANCH

M.R.

To Redditch
and Evesham

BROMSGROVE

FINSTALL

TUTNALL

BIRMINGHAM CANAL

AND

WORCESTER

Three Lines Junction (55ᵐ27ᶜ)
Bottom of Incline (55ᵐ28ᶜ)
STATION 144ᵐ79ᶜ (55ᵐ31ᶜ)
Station S.B. (55ᵐ33ᶜ)
Goods Lines Junction (55ᵐ35ᶜ)

WAGON REPAIRING WORKS

Altitude 257 feet

Hewell
Grange

South Junction S.B. (55ᵐ65ᶜ) Goods Lines Junction (55ᵐ64ᶜ)

STOKE PRIOR

M.R.

BIRMINGHAM & GLOUCESTER

This extract from a Midland Railway Distance
Diagram shows the line between Northfield and
Bromsgrove and part of the Halesowen branch from
Halesowen Junction to Rubery.

HALESOWEN JUNCTION

Ivatt Class 4MT No.43036 from 21A Saltley at the head of a down Ordinary passenger train on 18th June 1955. The signals were the Northfield up distants and Halesowen Junction up advanced starter and the Halesowen Junction down outer home. The interesting feature of this picture is that the signals were GWR and not LMS. Following nationalisation, the Western Regional boundary was at Selly Oak and King's Heath, but later it was cut back to Linthurst.

The Halesowen Junction signalman's view of the junction. This picture was taken on 29th July 1955 from the signal box and shows British Railways Standard Class 5MT No. 73054 running on the down slow line with an empty coaching stock train.

This c1953 picture depicts the open nature of the line near Barnt Green very well and shows a Birmingham New Street to Redditch Ordinary passenger train hauled by taper-boiler 2-6-2T No. 40099 approaching Barnt Green station.

The approach to Barnt Green from the north was on an embankment, and this picture of an unidentified Class 4F was taken in 1953 and shows a Class D express freight train on the down fast line approaching Barnt Green Mainline Junction. To the right we can see part of the sidings that were at this station.

The line towards Halesowen Junction from Barnt Green was on an embankment, as shown by this picture taken on 8th June 1954. The Express passenger train, headed by Class 5 No. 44945, would have started from Bristol and was probably going to Leeds or Bradford, but we cannot be certain of the final destination.

Ivatt Class 4MT 2-6-0s were often used to haul passenger trains in the Birmingham area and this picture, taken on 8th June 1953 from Barnt Green signal box, shows No. 43013 on an up Ordinary train running on the up fast line.

BARNT GREEN

The station at Barnt Green was opened on 1st May 1844 but on 1st June 1857 it became Barnt Green for Redditch. A few years later (about 1863,) the name of the station was altered to Barnt Green for Bromsgrove Lickey, but on 1st July 1868 it reverted to Barnt Green. It became a junction station when the Redditch Railway (opened for passengers on 19th September and goods on 1st October 1859) began to operate trains. The railway was leased to the Midland on incorporation and merged with effect from 1st January 1875. In this picture we can see the Birmingham end of Barnt Green station on 9th July 1955. Class 5 No. 45106 from 12A Carlisle Upperby was on a special train with a Western Division reporting number W726, running under express passenger train headcode, coming from the Redditch line.

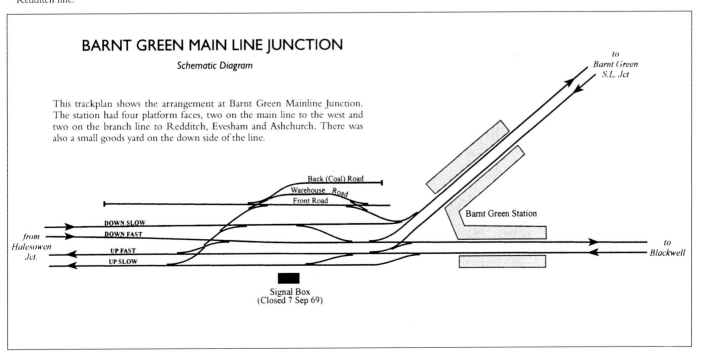

BARNT GREEN MAIN LINE JUNCTION

Schematic Diagram

This trackplan shows the arrangement at Barnt Green Mainline Junction. The station had four platform faces, two on the main line to the west and two on the branch line to Redditch, Evesham and Ashchurch. There was also a small goods yard on the down side of the line.

to
Barnt Green
S.L. Jct.

Back (Coal) Road
Warehouse Road
Front Road

DOWN SLOW
DOWN FAST
UP FAST
UP SLOW

from
Halesowen
Jct.

Barnt Green Station

to
Blackwell

Signal Box
(Closed 7 Sep 69)

The main line from Bromsgrove through Barnt Green was double track, but at the end of the platform there was a connection to the up slow line which continued to Halesowen Junction where it became a goods line. The connection to the branch to Redditch and beyond can be seen running from the centre of the picture to the lower right-hand corner. The signals on the left were: left arm to run onto the up slow line, and right arm to continue on the up fast line. The other bracket signal controlled trains from the branch; the left arm was for the up slow line and the right arm for the up fast line. Other connections that can be seen are from the down slow onto the down fast, and various ones between all running lines and the sidings seen at the right-hand side of the picture.

This picture was taken in 1953 from the end of the down main platform at Barnt Green. The approaching train, hauled by Class 5 No. 44841, was a westbound express, probably heading for Bristol, whilst the train on the right, headed by another Class 5, No. 44815, was standing on the branch up platform waiting for the road. At this date the use of a Class 5 on passenger trains on this line was somewhat unusual. Until the express has passed and the signals returned to normal, the road could not be set for the train from the Redditch branch.

A close-up of the bracket signal seen opposite. Although the routeing for the arms is given in that caption, it is worth repeating here. The left arm was for the up slow line to Halesowen Junction and the right-hand arm to continue along the up fast line. The reason for including this picture was to draw attention to the lower co-acting arms that enabled a driver to see what aspect was displayed as he approached from the west. Overleaf we show the footbridge and road bridge which were the reason for their installation; the bridges restricted the driver's view of the arms at the top of the post.

Barnt Green: station main line platforms as seen on 24th June 1961 looking towards Birmingham, with the signals seen earlier visible over the footbridge which connected all platforms.

This picture, taken on 20th April 1954, shows a west-bound, probably Washwood Heath to Westerleigh Class J mineral train, running through Barnt Green station towards Blackwell, the Lickey Incline and Bromsgrove.

This picture, taken on 20th April 1953, shows a Class 8F No. 48424 with a down Class J mineral train passing the Linthurst Intermediate Block signals. No. 48424 was one of the class 8s that were built at Swindon and ran on the GWR for a number of years.

The Class 4F 0-6-0s were employed on the Birmingham to Bristol line on various classes of express freight trains This picture shows No. 43946 with a down Class D semi-fitted freight train on 20th April 1954.

BLACKWELL

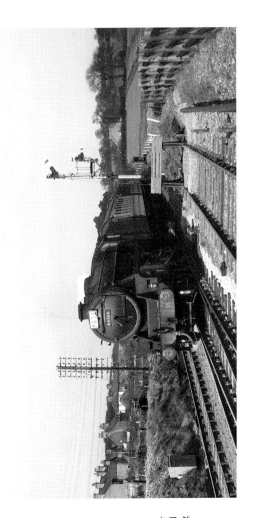

Class 5 No. 44984 with a down express carrying a reporting number M674 seen from the end of the down loop at Blackwell on 20th April 1954. The buffer stops at the end of the loop and part of the facing point that led from the down main to the loop can also be seen.

Class 4F No. 44201 from 21A Saltley leaving the down loop with it Class J mineral to run onto the Lickey incline, where the brakesman and guard would apply the required number of wagon hand brakes before the descent of the incline began. This photograph was taken on 20th April 1953.

Blackwell station was considered to be at the top of the Lickey incline; it was the point where the Bromsgrove bank engines ceased to give assistance to up trains. However, the actual summit at 563.87feet was close to Barnt Green and the main line continued to climb at 1 in 291 to the summit. The track layout was interesting. Running west from Birmingham, the down main line was straight, with a loop that would hold 70 wagons. This loop was the controlling factor for westbound goods trains. The maximum length of train allowed was equal to 60 in length, although it was extended from 23rd July 1967. Before this was done, the restriction meant that an engine, 60 wagons and a brakevan was all that could be accommodated in this loop and allow other trains to run past on the main line. In the up direction, the main line had been realigned to enable a centre bank engine siding to be laid. The conversion of the down refuge siding or layby came into use on 21st June 1931, and the bank engine siding from 27th April 1930. There was also an up loop that could hold 40 wagons and a goods yard with a capacity to hold 40 wagons. When this picture was taken from the up platform facing towards Birmingham in 1953, the approaching train was a Class J mineral hauled by Class 3F No. 43490, which would soon stop on the bank, where a number of wagon hand brakes would be applied before beginning the run to Bromsgrove.

Looking towards Birmingham on 13th March 1955, this picture shows the west end of the station where there was a siding behind the down platform, seen to the right of the picture.

This part interior view of Blackwell signal box, photographed on 20th April 1953, poses a question. What did the two wire-operated point levers work? There was a ground frame that was bolt locked from the signal box, but our information suggests that it was lever 33 that released the lock that enabled the levers in the ground frame to be pulled. These lever numbers appear to be 56 and 57; 56 was the facing point into the down loop and we cannot establish a function for lever 57.

On Sunday 6th and Sunday 13th March 1955, trials were held on the Lickey without bankers. On the first Sunday, Class 5 No. 44776 hauled a test train comprising six carriages plus a dynamometer car totalling 222 tons whilst the following Sunday Class 6P No. 45554 *Ontario* took a 252 ton train made up of seven carriages and a dynamometer car. The tests included standing starts on the 1 in 37.7 incline and runs at the bank. Although we do not have a picture of the Class 5, D.J.Norton photographed *Ontario* on the second Sunday and Class 4F No. 44092 returning down the bank with the test train.

It is rather difficult to explain what was happening when this picture was taken on 27th April 1949. The ascending express passenger train was being banked by 'The Banker', one of the names given to No. 2290, now renumbered 58100, but why wasn't the Class 3F tank engine buffered up to 58100? Normal practice was for the bank engines to remain buffered up until they reached Blackwell where the rear banker eased up and fell away from the train. On some occasions when there were three banking engines, the rear one dropped back from the train, then the second one, and finally the third. Returning down the incline, they were not coupled together. The leading engine's hand brake was applied and the regulator of the rear engine was opened, and this ensured that the engines remained buffered up on the descent to Bromsgrove South signal box where they returned to the bank engine sidings.

'Big Bertha', 'Big Emma', 'The Banker', were all nicknames given to the 0-10-0 that was built to bank trains up the Lickey Incline. This picture of No. 58100 banking a train up the incline was taken on 24th July 1949. If I may inject a personal note, I recall working to Bromsgrove one Saturday night in 1950 where we were relieved and sent home in the brakevan of a train heading for Washwood Heath. When we ascended the bank, my driver and the guard sat inside the brakevan, but I stood on the verandah just a few feet away from the smokebox of the banker as we went up the Lickey. The noise and experience were unforgettable.

'The Banker', photographed on 15th May 1949, buffered up to a passenger train prior to ascending the bank. The headlamp was very useful to the driver when it came to judging the distance from the rear of the train he was to assist up the Lickey Incline.

BROMSGROVE

This picture was taken from between the up main and up goods lines, looking towards Bromsgrove station and the Lickey incline on 31st May 1954. The water crane was used by enginemen to top up the tank prior to ascending the Lickey incline, whilst to the right 21C Bromsgrove engine shed is visible. The Class 5X at the head of the westbound express passenger train was No.45685 *Barfleur* emitting rather a lot of black smoke, not the sign of good firing!

Bromsgrove, facing the station with the incline beyond on 31st May 1954. Note the catch points on the down slow line to protect the connection from the down platform line and the down main line. Bromsgrove engine shed is seen to the right and the goods sidings to the left.

LONGBRIDGE TO HALESOWEN BRANCH

The line from Halesowen Junction (on the old Birmingham & Gloucester Railway) to an end-on junction with the GWR at Halesowen was worked jointly by the GWR and Midland, opening for goods and passenger traffic on 10th September 1883. On 1st July 1906 it was vested jointly in the Midland and Great Western companies. There were passenger stations at Longbridge, Rubery and Hunnington; the station at Halesowen was owned by the GWR. The joint line passenger stations at Rubery and Hun-

nington were closed for regular passenger traffic in April 1919, and Halesowen was closed for GWR public trains from Old Hill on 5th December 1927, but the passenger facilities at Longbridge, which started in February 1915, continued until 4th January 1960. Although the other stations were closed for regular passenger traffic, they remained open for workmen's trains, run in conjunction with the Austin Motor Works at Longbridge, which generated most of the freight traffic on the line.

HALESOWEN JUNCTION

Halesowen Junction marked the beginning of the Joint Midland & Great Western Railway line to Halesowen. The junction faced south from Birmingham and was one mile ten chains west of Northfield. This was taken facing west on 21st July 1956 and shows the up and down fast lines in the centre, with the up and down slow lines on the outside. The arrangements on the branch were rather different; there were in effect two single lines. The line close to the signal box was the main line and the line in the centre was the goods line, whilst, the line at the right-hand side of the picture was a short siding.

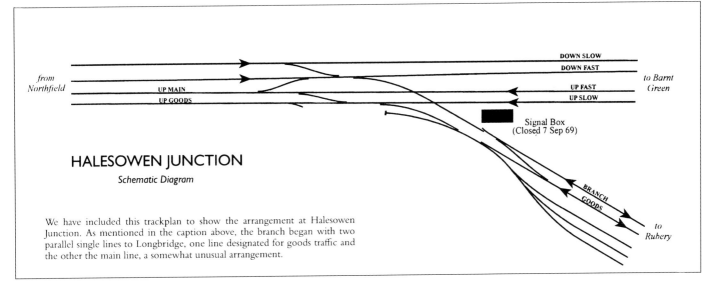

HALESOWEN JUNCTION
Schematic Diagram

We have included this trackplan to show the arrangement at Halesowen Junction. As mentioned in the caption above, the branch began with two parallel single lines to Longbridge, one line designated for goods traffic and the other the main line, a somewhat unusual arrangement.

Looking towards Northfield on 14th June 1954. At this point the slow lines from Barnt Green became goods lines to King's Norton and the goods line from King's Norton became a slow line to Barnt Green. Class 4F No. 44520 with a Class K Stopping freight train was running from the down goods line onto the Halesowen branch main line.

LONGBRIDGE

After the Austin Motor Car factory was established at Longbridge, this station became the terminating and originating point for most of the traffic on the Halesowen branch. This picture was taken on 12th March 1962 from alongside the 'south works', looking towards Longbridge station; the tall building in the centre of the picture was the station entrance on Bristol Road South, with Longbridge East Signal Box in front of the road bridge.

Later on the same day, 12th March 1962, this picture was taken looking towards Halesowen Junction and shows where the photographer was standing when the previous picture was taken. The pointwork was complex; the line to the left of the bracket signal post was the goods line and to the right the main line. The other lines were sidings connected to the Austin Motor Company's private railway.

Longbridge Lane pictured in March 1964. The small bridge seen to the right was close to Halesowen Junction. A much wider bridge was built parallel to the old one and, perhaps surprisingly, the original bridge was left in place rather than being demolished. The modern day Longbridge Station is now close to this site.

This picture was taken on 25th October 1961 from below South road bridge, looking towards Halesowen Junction. The running line next to the signal box was designated as a goods line and the one on the right the main line. Austin Motor Works was on both sides of the line and the footbridge was provided for the benefit of staff walking between the north and south works.

This view of Longbridge West signal box, taken on 12th March 1962 looking towards Rubery, also shows the sidings that were on the north side of the line.

This picture of Longbridge West signal box with the station beyond was taken on 12th March 1962 from the reception line alongside the single line to Halesowen, which is seen to the right. Part of Austin Motor Works can be seen in the background.

FROGMILL CROSSING

Frogmill Crossing was 29 chains east of Rubery station where there was a resident crossing keeper to open and close the gates. The distant signals seen on the top picture were somewhat unusual. The upper arm was the distant for Rubery and the lower arm was for Frogmill Crossing; the top arm was slotted by the bottom arm and could not be reversed unless the bottom arm had been pulled off. Note the nameboard in the lower picture to the left of the gates.

RUBERY STATION

This picture was taken on 8th July 1962 looking towards Longbridge with Rubery up starting signal, slotted by a lever in Frogmill Crossing ground frame seen in the distance. The main line is seen to the right and the line in the foreground was the beginning of the Birmingham Corporation's siding.

The second station along the line was Rubery where there was a quarry and connection to a private siding belonging to the Birmingham Corporation. This picture was taken on 12th July 1953 facing towards Longbridge at a point where there was a short siding that dealt with local coal traffic.

Although taken some time after the previous picture, on 8th July 1962, this shows to good effect the approach to Rubery from Longbridge. In the distance we can see Rubery signal box and station, and to the left the siding that was used for local coal traffic. Although the approach to Rubery from both Longbridge and Hunnington was single line, there were two running lines through the station. In this view we see the junction of the two lines and the catch point on the down line. Finally, on the far right, we can see part of the sidings that dealt with the quarry and Birmingham Corporation traffic.

This view of Rubery station, looking towards Halesowen, was taken from the 'four foot' of the down line on 11th July 1954. The road approach to the goods siding can be seen, together with the loading gauge to ensure any wagons loaded at Rubery were not out of gauge before they were despatched.

A post-1923 cast-iron notice board erected by the LM&S and GW Joint Lines.

This picture of Rubery was taken eight years later, on 8th July 1962, facing towards Halesowen Junction. As we can see, there were sidings on both sides of the line, but local traffic was almost non existent and, judging by the wagons that can be seen, was apparently confined to coal for domestic users.

A view of Rubery station on 31st May 1954 as seen from the Halesowen end of the station looking towards Halesowen Junction, with Holly Hill Crossing behind the photographer. The down starting signal can be seen at the end of the platform.

One feature of D.J Norton's photographs was his flexible approach to the interpretation of his lineside permit that was issued to enable him to take photographs. This picture was taken on 12th July 1953 from a goods brake van of a down goods train that was heading towards Halesowen, and illustrates the 17-lever signal box complete with signalman and his bicycle.

Holly Hill Crossing was on the Halesowen side of Rubery station, which can be seen in the distance. The signal was the up home signal; the down starting signal was on the platform and can be seen in a previous picture. The crossing gates were wire bolted by these signals which prevented them from being opened if either signal had been 'pulled off' for a train.

There were three over-bridges between Rubery station and Frankley sidings, this being the second one. This picture, taken on 29th May 1955, was looking towards Rubery with the Rubery distant visible through the arch.

The public sidings at Frankley were between Rubery and Hunnington, but when this picture was taken on 26th December 1954 there was no evidence of traffic, and the sidings were taken out of use in 1957. There were some complicated rules for working traffic to and from these sidings, access being obtained by the single-line token that released the ground frame which worked the points.

Dowery Dell viaduct was a rather spectacular sight between Frankley Public sidings and Hunnington station. Unfortunately, only a limited number of locomotive classes were allowed to work over it and it was this restriction that saw the retention of a few old Midland double-frame 0-6-0s at Bournville to work the goods traffic over the line. This picture was taken on 29th May 1955 with the Rubery end of the viaduct to the right of the picture.

Hunnington station was not a block post but there was a goods loop off the running line. The point levers in the ground frame, seen on the left, could be unlocked by using the key on the train staff. This picture was taken on 12th July 1953 when D.J.Norton was riding in a goods brake van.

The down home GWR signal marked the end of the joint line that was just before the railway entered Halesowen station.

Halesowen station, looking towards Hunnington and the joint line to Halesowen Junction on 7th October 1956. There were two platform faces at the station with a centre siding, but most of the passenger traffic was from Old Hill. The GWR opened the station for passenger traffic on 1st March 1878 and the Midland Railway on 10th September 1883. In April 1919 the Midland closed the station for ordinary passenger traffic, and the GWR closure for ordinary passenger traffic from Old Hill was on 5th March 1927. On 31st March 1928 the GWR began to run workmen's trains to Longbridge and they ceased to operate thirty years later on 1st September 1958.

At Barnt Green the branch to Redditch and Evesham curved away sharply to the left. I can recall Charlie Rae, my driver when I was in the 'Evesham Link', telling me that on the branch you could 'shake hands' with the guard in a number of places. Although this was an exaggeration, it was certainly true to say there were numerous curves on the line, and this picture provides readers with a good example of them. Reference to the distance diagram opposite will show how the line curved between Barnt Green and Redditch. This picture, taken on 9th July 1955, shows the two branch platforms at the station.

BARNT GREEN TO REDDITCH

Beyond the end of the branch platforms the double line became single, and this picture shows how the line continued to curve away from the station. The signal to the right was Barnt Green Single Line Junction starter and if this was clear, you could proceed to the end of the platform. If the distant below the stop signal was clear, the driver knew he had the road through Barnt Green onto the up fast line to Halesowen Junction, whilst the combination of the stop signal and left-hand distant (when facing the signal) told him he was going to run along the slow line from the junction towards Halesowen Junction.

The line between Barnt Green (on the old Birmingham & Gloucester Railway) and Redditch was opened for passengers on 19th September and for goods on 1st October 1859. By the time D. J. Norton began to take pictures, it was the north end of a railway that ran via Evesham to Ashchurch, where it rejoined the Birmingham & Gloucester line. The railway to Evesham was single line and Alvechurch was the only passenger station between Barnt Green and Redditch, opening on 1st November 1859. Redditch was one of the most important stations on the entire line and remains open today. Beyond Redditch, the line to Evesham was closed on 1st October 1962 and from Evesham to Ashchurch on 17th June 1963. The local industry at Redditch generated a reasonable amount of freight traffic, in particular for the gas works, and there was a small locomotive shed to the north of the station, which was a sub-shed of Bournville. The line was electrified and opened on 28th May 1993 as the southern end of the cross-city link to Lichfield, running via Bournville and New Street.

This extract taken from a Midland Railway Distance Diagram shows the branch line from the junction with the old Birmingham & Gloucester line to Redditch.

The Ivatt Class 4MTs were ideal locomotives for working on the Evesham branch and from the early days of British Railways began to be employed on the Birmingham to Ashchurch Ordinary passenger trains. This picture, taken on 9th July 1955, shows No. 43013, which was stationed at 21A Saltley, working an Ordinary passenger train that is seen approaching Barnt Green station.

The branch from Barnt Green to Redditch and Ashchurch via Evesham was 33 miles in length, with the busier northern section to Evesham mostly single line. At Barnt Green station there were up and down platforms for the branch trains, but beyond the Redditch end of the platforms the single lines began. This picture, taken on 2nd May 1953, shows the junction of the up and down lines and start of the single line at the appropriately named Barnt Green Single Line Junction signal box.

BARNT GREEN SINGLE LINE JUNCTION
Schematic Diagram

Barnt Green Single Line Junction marked the end of the double line from the junction and the start of the single line.

Signal Box
(Closed 7 Sep 69)

Although the branch was single line, a number of important freight trains ran over it. This picture, taken on 10th May 1954, shows one of Saltley's Horwich Moguls, that were better known as 'Crabs' passing Barnt Green Single Line Junction signal box where the fireman would surrender the tablet (see picture below). No. 42822 was working an express freight train that was probably heading for the goods station at Lawley Street or the marshalling sidings at Water Orton.

Between Redditch and Evesham the single line was worked by token, which was the driver's authority to be on a section of single line. Each token applied to a particular section and, when it was handed to the driver, it was in a leather pouch attached to what can only be described as a hoop. The signalman held the hoop so that the fireman leaning out of the cab could catch it. When firemen were exchanging tokens, that is surrendering the token for the section the train had already run along and collecting the token for the section ahead that the train was about to enter, the advice was to throw the hoop towards the signalman, but be careful not to hit him, but to ensure you collected the token for the new section. This picture was taken on 20th April 1954 and shows the fireman of a train heading towards Redditch collecting the token which authorised the train to be on the section to Redditch North signal box.

The Stanier Class 3P 2-6-2Ts were employed on the Birmingham New Street to Redditch passenger services. This picture was taken on 20th April 1954 and shows No. 40099 approaching Barnt Green with an Ordinary passenger train.

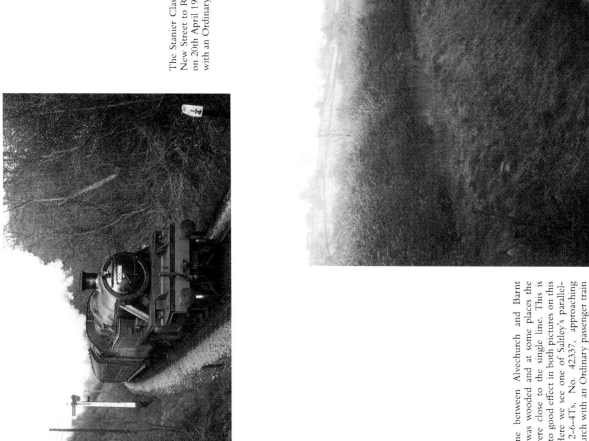

The line between Alvechurch and Barnt Green was wooded and at some places the trees were close to the single line. This is shown to good effect in both pictures on this page. Here we see one of Saltley's parallel-boiler 2-6-4Ts, No. 42337, approaching Alvechurch with an Ordinary passenger train heading for either Evesham or Ashchurch. Although a number of passenger trains from Birmingham terminated at Ashchurch, some only ran as far as Evesham; the majority worked between Birmingham and Redditch.

The only intermediate station between Barnt Green and Redditch was Alvechurch, which was opened for goods and passenger traffic on 1st November 1859. The station was not a block post and the goods facilities were a single siding that held 10 wagons and a small goods shed at the Barnt Green end of the station platform. Entry to the siding was by a lever stage that was released by the token. This view, taken on 20th April 1954 from Station Road bridge was looking towards Redditch.

Alvechurch station, photographed on 20th April 1954 from the end of the goods siding with Class 4F No. 44601 heading an up Class D semi-fitted express freight train towards Barnt Green.

Alvechurch on 20th April 1954, looking towards Barnt Green. The short siding, which had a side loading dock, can be seen but the goods shed was at the far end of the platform beyond the station building. The large building at the Redditch end of the platform was the stationmaster's house.

REDDITCH

The end of the single-line section was at Redditch North signalbox where the separate up and down lines began. The double line continued past the small engine shed, seen on the left, past goods sidings on both sides of the line and the connection to the gas works. Beyond the station at Redditch South signal box the line became single.

Parallel-boiler 2-6-4T No. 42327 at Redditch engine shed on 22nd April 1951. The original shed received a new roof c1938, but the allocation was small, probably two locomotives. It was subshed of 21B Bournville; there was a small coal stage but there was no turntable. The view on the opposite page shows the water crane, ashpit and small hut that would have served as the messroom and stores.

During the period when D.J.Norton was taking pictures, Redditch was a most interesting place as far as traffic working was concerned, but with the closure of the line beyond Redditch, it became simply the southern terminus of the Cross City line. We have included this diagram to show the track layout at both the north and south ends of the station before closure took place.

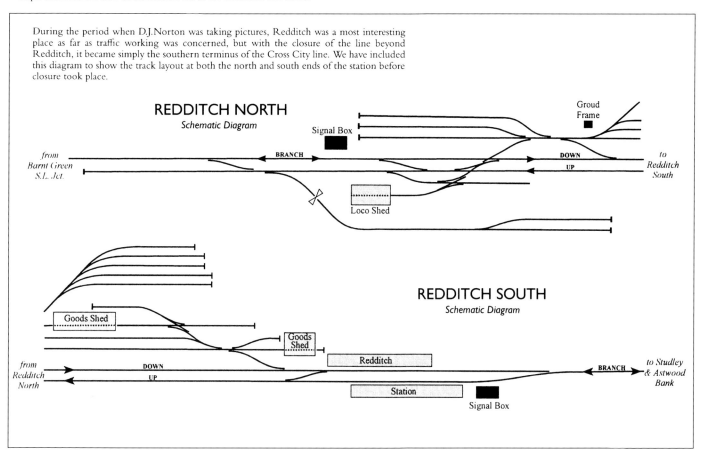

Looking towards Redditch tunnel from Redditch South signal box, on 12th July 1955. From an engineman's point of view, the single-line narrow bore was not a pleasant place, and if the engine was running quickly with the front damper open, it was possible to get a 'blow-back' and a flame of fire would come out of the firebox door into the cab. Therefore, firemen on the up line always closed the front damper as they approached the tunnel and the enginemen would not stand in front of the firedoors.

This picture was taken at Redditch South signal box on 12th July 1955, with Class 5 No. 44859 passing with a Class H Through freight train. Note the signalman standing on the platform used when tokens were to be surrendered, in readiness to receive the 'hoop' with the token in the pouch.